Sticky Icky Booger Bugs

SHERRY FRITH

illustrated By Carol Newell Walter

 ARCHWAY
PUBLISHING

Archway Publishing books may be ordered through booksellers or by
contacting:

Archway Publishing
1663 Liberty Drive
Bloomington, IN 47403
www.archwaypublishing.com
1-(888)-242-5904

ISBN: 978-1-4808-0083-0 (sc)
ISBN: 978-1-4808-0082-3 (e)

Printed in the United States of America

Archway Publishing rev. date: 07/26/2013

Dedicated with love to Kevin and Kory

Special thanks to Dr. William Baker,
Dr. Andres Gelrud, Dr. Jose Martinez,
Dr. Jose Quiros, Dr. Reddivalam Sudhakar,
Dr. Kevin Shannon, and Dr. Arron Banks

Preface

Sherry Frith wrote *Sticky Icky Booger Bugs* after her sons Kory and Kevin were diagnosed with cystic fibrosis. She wanted to give them a gift and an explanation for what they were facing in terms they could understand. Keeping the sticky icky booger bugs away became an important daily routine that kept the disease under control and her boys out of the hospital.

My name is Kory, and sticky icky booger bugs are part of my everyday life.

They try to stay in me, and I try to sneeze and cough them out.

I was diagnosed with cystic fibrosis when I was four years old.

So each morning, I wake up coughing
and sneezing out sticky icky booger bugs.

There are good days and bad days.

But every day I do my medicine routine
to keep the sticky icky booger bugs away.

I take two puffs of my blue inhaler—

squeeze, hold, inhale, wait, and breathe.

My mommy puts the shaker on me for thirty minutes. The doctors call it the life vest.

I call it the shaker because it shakes, shakes, shakes, and shakes some more.

All that shaking helps loosen up the
sticky icky booger bugs.
This can be really boring.

My mommy keeps me entertained with books, video games,
and DVDs. Sometimes my two brothers are entertainment
enough.

After what feels like forever, I am finished shaking.
Hip, hip, hooray!

Two puffs of my purple inhaler—squeeze, hold, inhale, wait,
and breathe—and more sticky icky booger bugs are coughed
up and out.

My mommy says to me all the time,

"Better out than in.
You don't want an
infection, do you, Kory?"

I do the normal things that every boy and girl does. I get dressed, I wash, and I comb my hair.

I have to brush my teeth a lot because of the medication from my blue and purple inhalers.

At breakfast, my mommy places my pep and
gas-attack pills on my napkin to take with my pancakes.

I love to drink a big glass of chocolate milk
with my breakfast too.

Pep pills are an enzyme that I take with my meals and snacks.

It helps my stomach break up the food so my tummy won't hurt. The gas-attack pills help with my burping and tooting.

I love to snack all day long.

But whenever I snack, I have to remember
to take my pep pill.

At school, I go to the office and nurse Angie gives me my medication at lunch and snack time.

I like her. She is very nice to me.

I get special attention from my teachers because of my sticky icky booger bugs.

They let me drink a juice box during class because it's not good for my body to lose a lot of water or salt.

At recess I play just like everyone else. I love to skip, run, and jump.

My favorite thing is to play soccer with my friends.

When I come home from school, my mommy makes me do my shaker right away. So out come the inhalers and smoker.

The smoker is a nebulizer machine that is used to give me a salt solution through an inhaler.

My mommy tells me to breathe in and to not let the smoke come out of my nose.

I can sometimes be stubborn, and she has to put the nose clip on to make sure all the medicine stays in.

I shake, breathe in my medicine, and entertain myself with a video game.

While I shake out the sticky icky booger bugs, my mommy makes me a good snack. She also gives me my pep pill.

After I finish my homework, I go outside to play with my best friend, Cody.

Our favorite thing to do is explore our neighborhood. We like to dress up in costumes and pretend.

Then it's off to the shower to clean out my sticky icky booger bugs again.

I have a salt wash in the shower. Spraying this up my nose makes me think of the beach.

Soon I will have the sticky icky booger bugs slipping out of my nose.

A couple of *achoos* and I am breathing better.

If we eat dinner at home or at a restaurant, my mommy always carries my pep pills.

My treat at night is usually a cup of ice cream. Mommy puts my vitamin in it, and it slides right down the hatch.

Bedtime is what I like best. My mommy will always lie down with me and rub my back.

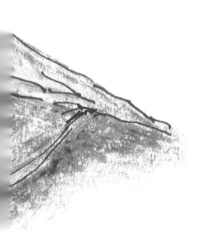

She tells me how special I am and how much she loves me just as I am.

Afterword

After being diagnosed in 2010 with a rare genetic heart condition, Sherry's future was unknown. She made the decision to leave something for her boys, and this book unfolded with the help of her neighbor Carol, who created the illustrations and whose grandson is also in the story. Kory's story reminds him and other children that they are special.

About the Author

About the Illustrator

Sherry is the mother of three boys and the founder of a non-profit organization called KCHH, Inc. She has patents and copyrights pending in different areas and lives each day full of new ideas and grace. Sherry lives in Bakersfield, California, with her three boys, Kyle, Kevin, and Kory.

Carol Newell Walter was born in Chicago, Illinois. She majored in Fine Arts at Wayne State University. She has a BA and teaching credential from California State University Bakersfield. Now retired, Carol continues to enjoy creating all kinds of artwork. Carol and her husband, Gordon, live in Bakersfield, California.

CPSIA information can be obtained at www.ICGtesting.com
Printed in the USA
LVIW01n1015161017
552599LV00003B/14